UZBEKISTAN 2016 HUMAN RIGHTS REPORT

EXECUTIVE SUMMARY

Uzbekistan is an authoritarian state with a constitution that provides for a presidential system with separation of powers among the executive, legislative, and judicial branches. The executive branch under former President Islam Karimov dominated political life and exercised nearly complete control over the other branches of government. On September 2, President Karimov died in office and new elections took place on December 4. Former prime minister Shavkat Mirziyoyev won with 88 percent of the vote. The Organization for Security and Cooperation's Office for Democratic Institutions and Human Rights (OSCE/ODHIR), in its preliminary election observation mission report, noted that "limits on fundamental freedoms undermine political pluralism and led to a campaign devoid of genuine competition." The report also identified positive changes such as the election's increased transparency, service to disabled voters, and unfettered access for 600 international observers.

Civilian authorities generally maintained effective control over the security forces, but security services permeated civilian structures, and their interaction was opaque, which made it difficult to define the scope and limits of civilian authority.

The most significant human rights problems included torture and abuse of detainees by security forces, denial of due process and fair trial, and an inability of citizens to choose their government in free, fair, and periodic elections.

Other continuing human rights problems included incommunicado and prolonged detention; harsh and sometimes life-threatening prison conditions; arbitrary arrest and detention; and widespread restrictions on religious freedom, including harassment of religious minority group members and continued imprisonment of believers of all faiths. Problems also included restrictions on freedom of speech, press, assembly, and association; restrictions on civil society; restrictions on freedom of movement; violence against women; the inability of citizens to obtain adequate social services such as public health and education; and human trafficking, including government-compelled forced labor. There was widespread disregard for the rule of law as authorities subjected human rights activists, journalists, and others who criticized the government, as well as their family members, to harassment, arbitrary arrest, physical abuse, and politically motivated prosecution and detention.

Government prosecutions of officials were rare, selective, but often public, and officials frequently engaged in corrupt practices with impunity.

Section 1. Respect for the Integrity of the Person, Including Freedom from:

a. Arbitrary Deprivation of Life and other Unlawful or Politically Motivated Killings

There were reports that the government or its agents committed arbitrary or unlawful killings, including by torture.

In February, Ozodlik Radio, the Uzbek Service of Radio Free Europe/Radio Liberty (RFE/RL), reported that police brought the body of Makhmudjon Khasanov, who was serving a prison term at penal colony No. 64/46 in Navoi for affiliation with the banned religious organization Hizb-ut-Tahrir, to his family without official forensic medical examination records of the detainee's death. Police demanded immediate burial. According to Fergana News, the death resulted from torture.

Information regarding other deaths from torture was not available, however, other reported cases that fit this pattern included the deaths of Doston Abdurakhmanov, Shakhob Makhkamov, and Ikromjon Nizamov in February.

b. Disappearance

There were no reports of politically motivated disappearances, although some prisoners' family members reported being unable to locate their relatives when attempting to visit them in penitentiary systems.

In its 2016 annual report, the Geneva based UN Working Group on Enforced or Involuntary Disappearances noted it had seven outstanding cases from previous years. According to the working group, the government did not respond to the group's requests to visit the country, and the information provided by the government was insufficient to clarify the status of the seven outstanding cases.

There were reports that persons sought by the country's law enforcement bodies were abducted abroad by the country's secret services, with the acquiescence or direct cooperation of national and multilateral security structures abroad, even when granted asylum status, and were forcibly returned to the country to stand trial.

Lawyers for Rakhmiddin Kamolov reported an attempt to kidnap their client on August 29 in Moscow. Kamolov was wanted in Uzbekistan on charges of affiliating with a banned religious organization. According to reports from the Moscow-based Yordam (Help) Consulting-Legal Center, the Uzbek National Security Service (NSS) kidnapped Kamolov, exposed him to physical and psychological abuse, and later that same day forcibly transported him to the airport for return to Uzbekistan. Russian authorities intervened, took Kamolov into custody, and later released him. He remained in Russia awaiting a decision by Russian authorities on Uzbekistan's extradition request.

c. Torture and Other Cruel, Inhuman, or Degrading Treatment or Punishment

While the constitution and law prohibit such practices, law enforcement and security officers routinely beat and otherwise mistreated detainees to obtain confessions, incriminating information, or for corrupt financial gain. Sources reported torture and abuse were common in prisons, pretrial facilities, and local police and security service precincts. Reported methods of torture included severe beatings, denial of food, simulated asphyxiation, tying and hanging by the hands, and electric shock. There were also continued reports that authorities exerted psychological pressure on inmates and detainees, including through threats against family members and blackmail.

In 2010 the UN Human Rights Committee expressed concern that the definition of torture in the criminal code did not conform to the Convention against Torture and Other Cruel, Inhuman, or Degrading Treatment or Punishment, to which the country is a party. The most recent country assessment by the UN special rapporteur on torture and other cruel, inhuman, or degrading treatment or punishment was in 2003, as the country has not responded to subsequent requests for this or any other UN special rapporteur to visit since 2002.

On February 19, the Jizzakh Regional Criminal Court sentenced five men--Aramais Avakyan, Furkat Djuraev, Bektemir Umirzokov, Akmal Mamatmurodov, and Dilshod Alimov--to prison terms ranging from seven to 12 years for criminal charges against the state related to terrorism, attempts to overthrow the state; production and distribution of materials containing threats to public security and public order; and the creation, leadership, and participation in religious extremist, separatist, fundamentalist and other banned organizations. During the court hearing, Avakyan and others reported that Jizzakh regional NSS and police officers used torture to extract false confessions. In response to questions regarding the case, the government denied this account and stated that an internal investigation found the torture claims groundless.

On March 7, Elena Urlaeva, chairperson of the Human Rights Alliance of Uzbekistan, was forcibly placed in a psychiatric hospital, according to a decision from the Mirabad Inter-District Court. After her release on June 2, Urlaeva reported that during her incarceration at Tashkent City Psychiatric Hospital No. 1, authorities beat her on numerous occasions and forcefully gave her psychotropic substances. Hospital authorities refused to perform any medical examinations to confirm or deny claims of mistreatment or conduct a blood analysis, as requested. Authorities also hospitalized Urlaeva in 2001, 2002, 2005, and 2012 following reports of her activism.

Authorities reportedly increased the severity of punishments for individuals suspected of "Islamist extremism." Local human rights workers reported that authorities often proffered inducements--such as bribes or prison privileges--to inmates who agreed to harass and harm other inmates suspected of "religious extremism." The government does not differentiate between violent and nonviolent forms of extremism.

Prison and Detention Center Conditions

Prison conditions were in some circumstances harsh and life threatening.

<u>Physical Conditions</u>: There were reports that, in some facilities, inmates convicted of attempting to overthrow the constitutional order were held separately, and that prison officials isolated inmates convicted under "religious extremism" charges from other inmates, according to human rights monitors.

Reports of overcrowding, severe abuse, and shortages of medicine were common. Inmates generally had access to potable water and food, but both reportedly were of poor quality. Relatives of prisoners sometimes complained that prison diets did not include sufficient meat. There were reports of political prisoners held in cells without proper ventilation and subjected to temperatures below freezing in winter and over 120 degrees in summer; detention facilities commonly lacked heat or air conditioning. Family members also reported occasions when officials withheld or delayed delivery of food and medicine intended for prisoners. Unlike in past years, family members of inmates did not report any incidents of sexual abuse.

Prison administration officials reported an active World Health Organization tuberculosis program in the prisons and an HIV/AIDS treatment and prevention program. Officials reported hepatitis was not present in high numbers and that hepatitis patients received treatment in existing medical facilities and programs. Reports of such treatment could not be verified independently because access to such facilities was frequently denied.

Administration: There was no information available whether recordkeeping on prisoners was adequate. Authorities in limited cases used administrative measures such as bail, house arrest and correctional work as alternatives to criminal sentences for nonviolent offenders. In addition, the criminal code mandates instances in which courts cannot sentence individuals to prison if he or she has paid a fine in full.

The Human Rights Ombudsman's office and the Prosecutor General's Office may investigate complaints from detainees. The Ombudsman's Office may make recommendations on behalf of specific prisoners, including changes to the sentences of nonviolent offenders to make them more appropriate to the offense. The Ombudsman's Office noted, however, that it rarely received complaints from prisoners regarding detention conditions. Family members of detained or released prisoners said their complaints to the ombudsman went unanswered or were referred to the original sentencing court for redress without investigation from the ombudsman.

Prison officials generally allowed family members to visit prisoners for up to four hours two to four times per year. Relatives of prisoners held on religious or extremism charges reported denial of visitation rights. Officials also permitted longer visits of one to three days two to four times per year, depending on the type of prison facility. Family members of political prisoners reported that officials frequently delayed or severely shortened visits arbitrarily. Family members of other prisoners mentioned that visits were often conditional on payment of a bribe to officials.

The government stated prisoners have the right to practice any religion or no religion, but prisoners frequently complained to family members that they were not able to observe religious rituals conflicting with the prison's schedule. Such rituals included traditional Islamic morning prayers. Authorities forbid prisoners to observe religious holidays such as Ramadan, with no fasting allowed. Although some prison libraries had copies of the Quran and the Bible, family members continued to complain that authorities did not allow prisoners access to religious materials.

According to official government procedures, prisoners have the right to "participate in religious worship and family relations, such as marriage." "Close relatives" also have the right to receive oral and written information from prison officials about the health and disciplinary records of their family members. Families continued to report a lack of communication and information concerning their imprisoned relatives and stated that the government continued to withhold information contained in health and prison records.

According to family members and nongovernmental organizations (NGOs), authorities at times failed to release prisoners, especially those convicted of "religious extremism," at the end of their terms. Prison authorities often extended inmates' terms by accusing them of additional crimes or of violating vague or internal prison rules or claiming the prisoners represented a continuing danger to society.

Authorities extended the sentences of human rights activist Ganikhon Mamatkhanov by an additional three years in May and opposition activist Samandar Kukanov by an additional five years in October, reportedly for violations of internal prison rules. The government subsequently released Kukanov in November under its annual amnesty program.

Independent Monitoring: Independent observers had limited access to some parts of the penitentiary system, including pretrial detention facilities, juvenile and women's prisons, and prison settlements. Authorities granted access to selected observers, but only to certain prisons and to limited areas within them. On July 20, authorities allowed local human rights activists from the Ezgulik Human Rights Society to visit Mukhammad Bekjanov at prison No. 64/48, Zarafshan District, Navoi region; Azam Farmonov at prison No. 64/71, Jaslyk, Karakalpakstan; and Isroil Kholdorov, at prison No. 64/29, Navoi. No UN rapporteurs or representatives from the international community were allowed to visit prisons during the year.

d. Arbitrary Arrest or Detention

The constitution and the law prohibit arbitrary arrest and detention, but authorities continued to engage in such practices.

Role of the Police and Security Apparatus

The government authorizes three different entities to investigate criminal activity. The Ministry of Interior controls the police, who are responsible for law enforcement, maintenance of order, and the investigation of general crimes. The Prosecutor General's Office investigates violent crimes such as homicide as well as corruption by officials and abuse of power. The NSS, headed by a chairman who reports directly to the president, deals with national security and intelligence problems, including terrorism, corruption, organized crime, border control, and narcotics. When jurisdictions overlap, the agencies determine among themselves, which takes the lead.

Impunity was a problem. The Ministry of Interior investigated abuses but rarely disciplined officers accused of human rights violations. A human rights and legal education department within the ministry investigated some police brutality cases. The Human Rights Ombudsman's Office, affiliated with parliament, also has the power to investigate cases, although its decisions on such investigations have no binding authority.

Arrest Procedures and Treatment of Detainees

By law a judge must review any decision to arrest accused individuals or suspects. Judges granted arrest warrants in most cases. Defendants have the right to legal counsel from the time of arrest. State-appointed attorneys are available for those who do not hire private counsel. Officials did not always respect the right to counsel and occasionally forced defendants to sign written statements declining the right. Authorities' selective intimidation and disbarment of defense lawyers produced a chilling effect that also compromised political detainees' access to legal counsel. The law authorizes the use of house arrest as a form of pretrial detention.

Detainees have the right to request hearings before a judge to determine whether they remain incarcerated or may be released before trial. The arresting authority is required to notify a relative of a detainee about the detention and to question the detainee within 24 hours of arrest. There were complaints that authorities tortured suspects before notifying either family members or attorneys of their arrest to gain confessions that could be used for convictions.

Suspects have the right to remain silent and must be informed of the right to counsel. Detention without formal charges is limited to 72 hours, although a prosecutor can request an additional 48 hours, after which time the person must be charged or released. Authorities typically held suspects after the allowable period of detention, according to human rights advocates. After formal charges are filed, the prosecutor decides whether a suspect is released on bail (or on the guarantee of an individual or public organization acting as surety), stays in pretrial detention, or is kept under house arrest. The judge conducting the arrest hearing is allowed to sit on the panel of judges during the individual's trial.

The law requires authorities at pretrial detention facilities to arrange a meeting between a detainee and a representative from the Human Rights Ombudsman's Office upon the detainee's request. Officials allowed detainees in prison facilities to submit confidential complaints to the Ombudsman's Office and the Prosecutor General's Office.

Once authorities file charges, suspects may be held in pretrial detention for up to three months while investigations proceed. The law permits an extension of the investigation period for as much as one year at the discretion of the appropriate court upon a motion by the relevant prosecutor, who may also release a prisoner on bond pending trial. According to human rights advocates, authorities frequently ignored these legal protections. Those arrested and charged with a crime may be released without bail until trial on the condition they provide assurance of "proper behavior" and that they will appear at trial.

A decree requires that all defense attorneys pass a comprehensive relicensing examination. Several experienced and knowledgeable defense lawyers who had represented human rights activists and independent journalists lost their licenses after taking the relicensing examination or because of letters from the bar association under the control of the Ministry of Justice claiming that they violated professional ethical norms. As a result several activists and defendants faced difficulties in finding legal representation. Although unlicensed advocates cannot represent individuals in criminal and civil hearings, courts have the discretion to allow such an advocate if he or she belongs to a registered organization whose members are on trial.

Arbitrary Arrest: Authorities continued to arrest or detain persons arbitrarily on charges of extremist sentiments or activities and association with banned religious groups. Local human rights activists reported that police and security service officers, acting under pressure to break up extremist cells, frequently detained and mistreated family members and close associates of suspected members of religious extremist groups. Coerced confessions and testimony in such cases were commonplace.

On January 20, seven police and security services officers detained Sharufitdin Tashpulatov in the Mirzo-Ulugbek district of Tashkent on hooliganism charges. The Mirzo-Ulugbek Criminal Court sentenced him to 15 days of incarceration, during which Tashpulatov was severely abused to confess to religious offenses. In 1999 Tashpulatov was sentenced and served nine years in prison for membership in the banned religious organization Hizb-ut-Tahrir and for attempting to overthrow constitutional order, among other charges.

In November 2015 authorities arrested human rights activist Uktam Pardaev following a search of his house. Pardaev faced criminal charges, including conspiracy to swindle and offer bribes, which carried maximum penalties of up to 10 years' imprisonment. On January 11, Pardaev was convicted on all charges, sentenced to almost eight years in prison, and then immediately exonerated and released with the informal warning that he may not engage in human rights-related activities for three years.

There were reports that police detained persons on false charges of extortion, drug possession, tax evasion, or extremism as an intimidation tactic to prevent them or their family members from exposing corruption or interfering in local criminal activities. On April 22, in Gurlan District, Khorezm Province, Valibek Eshmanov was forcibly removed from a taxi after witnessing and commenting on a traffic police officer's demand and acceptance of a bribe. He was beaten severely on the street and transported to the district police station on charges of obstructing justice. The Gurlan District Court convicted Eshmanov and fined him one day's pay. Eshmanov was later exonerated in a general amnesty, but his police record prevented him from obtaining meaningful employment. Eshmanov filed repeated requests with the Office of the Ombudsman, Supreme Court, President's Office, Prosecutor General's Office as well as law enforcement bodies, alleging his innocence and the misconduct of police. At year's end Eshmanov had not received a reply to his request for judicial review of his case and expunging of his criminal record.

Pretrial Detention: Prosecutors generally exercised discretion over most aspects of criminal procedures, including pretrial detention. Detainees had no access to a court to challenge the length or validity of pretrial detention. Even when authorities did not file charges, police and prosecutors frequently sought to evade restrictions on the length of time persons could be held without charges by holding them as witnesses rather than as suspects. Pretrial detention ranged from one to three months. The government did not provide information regarding the number of persons held in pretrial detention centers.

Detainees or former detainees are able to challenge the lawfulness of their detention before a court. Appeals are sometimes open to the public by request of the applicant and new evidence rarely heard. Appeal courts generally review previous trial records and ask applicants to declare for the record their innocence or guilt. Appeals rarely result in the courts overturning their original decisions.

Detainee's Ability to Challenge Lawfulness of Detention before a Court: Detainees or former detainees are able to challenge the lawfulness of their detention before a court. Appeals are sometimes open to the public by request of the applicant and new evidence rarely heard. Appeal courts generally review previous trial records and ask applicants to declare for the record their innocence or guilt. Appeals rarely result in the courts overturning their original decisions.

Amnesty: Authorities give amnesty and release some individuals imprisoned for religious extremism or political grounds every year. In November 2015 Murod Juraev was released after 21 years in prison. Juraev, a former member of parliament and opposition figure, was sentenced in 1994 to 12 years, which was extended in 2003, 2006, 2009, and 2012, allegedly for violations of internal prison rules. Following his release, Juraev remained on parole for one year and reported regularly to police authorities who detained him--and at times his wife--for up to six hours without food, water, or bathroom access. No explanations were provided, but detentions occurred when members of the diplomatic corps attempted to visit him.

Released in October, Bobomurod Razzokov, a farmer and head of the Ezgulik human rights organization, was sentenced to four years in prison on accusations of facilitating the trafficking of a woman into prostitution in 2013. Razzokov's lawyer claimed that security services pressured the woman into bringing charges against him. The 60-year-old maintained that the charges were politically motivated due to his human rights activities, and human rights organizations alleged serious due process violations.

In November, the government amnestied and released political prisoner Samandar Kukanov. Kukanov, a former member of parliament and businessman, was sentenced to 20 years in prison in July 1993. In 2013, his prison term was prolonged for three years for violating internal prison rules. His sentence was extended again in October, shortly before the government granted him amnesty.

e. Denial of Fair Public Trial

Although the constitution provides for an independent judiciary, members of the judiciary reportedly rendered verdicts desired by the Prosecutor General's Office or other law enforcement bodies.

The president appoints all judges for renewable five-year terms. Removal of Supreme Court judges must be confirmed by parliament, which generally complied with the president's wishes.

Trial Procedures

The criminal code specifies a presumption of innocence. Most trials were officially open to the public, although access was sometimes restricted. Judges may close trials in exceptional cases, such as those involving state secrets or to protect victims and witnesses. Judges generally permitted international observers at proceedings without requiring written permission from the Supreme Court or court chairman, but judges or other officials arbitrarily closed some proceedings to observers, even in civil cases. Authorities generally announced trials only one or two days before they began, and hearings were frequently postponed.

A panel of one professional judge and two lay assessors, selected by committees of worker collectives or neighborhood committees, generally presided over trials. The lay judges rarely spoke, and the professional judge usually accepted prosecutors' recommendations on procedural rulings and sentencing.

Defendants have the right to attend court proceedings, confront witnesses, and present evidence, but judges declined defense motions to summon additional witnesses or to enter evidence supporting the defendant into the record. In the overwhelming majority of criminal cases brought to trial, the verdict was guilty. Defendants have the right to hire an attorney, and the system worked reasonably well, although some human rights activists encountered difficulties finding legal representation. The government provided legal counsel and interpreters without charge when necessary. According to credible reports, state-appointed defense attorneys routinely acted in the interest of the government rather than of their clients because of their reliance on the state for a livelihood and fear of possible recriminations, including nonrenewal of licenses.

By law a prosecutor must request an arrest order from a court, and courts rarely denied such requests. Prosecutors have considerable power after obtaining an arrest order: They direct investigations, prepare criminal cases, recommend sentences to judges, and may appeal court decisions, including the sentence. After formal charges are filed, the prosecutor decides whether a suspect is released on bail, stays in pretrial detention, or is kept under house arrest. Although the criminal code specifies a presumption of innocence, a prosecutor's recommendations generally prevailed. If a judge's sentence does not correspond with the prosecutor's recommendation, the prosecutor may appeal the sentence to a higher court. Judges often based their verdicts solely on confessions and witness testimony, which authorities were known to extract through abuse, threats to family members, or other means of coercion. This was especially common in religious extremism cases. Lawyers may, and occasionally did, call on judges to reject confessions and investigate claims of torture. Judges often did not respond to such claims or dismissed them as groundless. Courts failed to investigate properly allegations of torture. Judicial verdicts frequently alleged that defendants claimed torture to avoid criminal responsibility.

Legal protections against double jeopardy were not applied.

The law provides a right of appeal to defendants, but appeals rarely resulted in reversals of convictions. In some cases, however, appeals resulted in reduced or suspended sentences.

Defense attorneys may access government-held evidence relevant to their clients' cases after the initial investigation is completed, the prosecutor files formal charges, and the case is passed to the criminal court, except when the release of certain evidence could pose a threat to state security. In the past courts invoked the state security exception, leading to complaints that its primary purpose was to allow prosecutors to avoid sharing evidence with defense attorneys. In many cases prosecution was based solely upon defendants' confessions or incriminating testimony from state witnesses, particularly in cases involving alleged religious extremism.

Political Prisoners and Detainees

International and domestic human rights organizations estimated that authorities held hundreds of prisoners on political grounds, and some groups asserted the number was in the thousands. These claims were not statistically and independently verifiable. The government denied it held political prisoners and maintained that these individuals were convicted of violating the law. Officials released one high-profile prisoner, Bobomurod Razzokov, in October and another, Samandar Kukanov in November. Family members of several political prisoners, including Azam Farmonov, reported abuse in prison and deterioration of the prisoners' health.

Civil Judicial Procedures and Remedies

Citizens may file suit in civil courts for alleged human rights violations by officials, excluding investigators, prosecutors, and judges. There were reports that bribes to judges influenced civil court decisions.

f. Arbitrary or Unlawful Interference with Privacy, Family, Home, or Correspondence

Although the constitution and law forbids arbitrary or unlawful interference with privacy, family, home, or correspondence, authorities did not respect these prohibitions. The law requires that prosecutors approve requests for search warrants for electronic surveillance, but there is no provision for judicial review of such warrants.

There were reports that police and other security forces entered the homes of human rights activists and members of religious groups without a warrant. According to Forum 18, a Norwegian NGO that reports on religious freedom, members of Baptist, Jehovah's Witnesses, and other minority churches holding worship services in private homes reported that armed security officers raided services and detained and fined church members for religious activity deemed illegal. Among such incidents were raids in Khorezm in February and May. Baptist congregants reported home intrusions by authorities even when they gathered to celebrate important occasions such as birthdays. They also reported harassment and interference by authorities when publicly reading the Bible.

Human rights activists and political opposition figures generally assumed that security agencies covertly monitored their telephone calls and activities.

The government continued to use an estimated 12,000 neighborhood (mahalla) committees as a source of information on potential "extremists." The committees provided various social support functions, but they also functioned as an informational link from local society to government and law enforcement. Mahallas in rural areas tended to be more influential than those in cities.

There continued to be credible reports that police, employers, and mahalla committees harassed family members of human rights activists, such as Elena Urlaeva, Malokhat Eshonkulova, Uktam Pardaev, Gulshan Karaeva, and Chamangul Negmanova.

Section 2. Respect for Civil Liberties, Including:

a. Freedom of Speech and Press

The constitution and law provide for freedom of speech and press, but the government did not respect these rights and severely limited freedom of expression.

Freedom of Speech and Expression: The law restricts criticism of the president, and publicly insulting the president is a crime punishable by up to five years in prison. The law specifically prohibits publication of articles that incite religious confrontation and ethnic discord or that advocate subverting or overthrowing the constitutional order.

On April 25, the president signed an amendment criminalizing a broad range of religious expression online and via mass media. Criminal Code Article 244-1 (Threats to Public Security and Public Order) prescribes up to eight years in prison for anyone who uses religion online, via mass media, or in telecommunications to "violate civil concord, disseminate defamatory, destabilizing fabrications, commit other acts aimed against the established rules of behavior in society and public safety, and spread panic among the population." Anyone distributing or displaying "attributes and symbols of religious extremist and terrorist organizations" can face up to five years in prison.

Press and Media Freedoms: All media entities, foreign and domestic, must register with authorities and provide the names of their founder, chief editor, and staff members. Print media must also provide hard copies of publications to the government. The law holds all foreign and domestic media organizations accountable for the accuracy of their reporting, prohibits foreign journalists from working in the country without official accreditation, and subjects foreign media outlets to domestic mass media laws. The government used accreditation rules to deny foreign journalists and media outlets the opportunity to work in the country.

Amendments to the Law on Information Technologies, signed in September 2015, hold bloggers legally accountable for the accuracy of what they post and prohibit posts potentially perceived as defaming an individual's "honor and dignity." Limitations also preclude perceived calls for public disorder, encroachment on constitutional order, posting pornography or state secrets, issuing "threats to the state," and "other activities that are subject to criminal and other types of responsibilities according to legislation."

The government prohibited the promotion of religious extremism, separatism, and fundamentalism as well as the instigation of ethnic and religious hatred. It prohibited legal entities with more than 30 percent foreign ownership from establishing media outlets in the country.

Articles in state-controlled newspapers reflected the government's viewpoint. The main government newspapers published selected international wire stories. The government allowed publication of a few private newspapers with limited circulation containing advertising, horoscopes, and some substantive local news, including infrequent stories critical of government socioeconomic policies.

The government used large-circulation tabloids, such as *Darakchi* and *Bekajon*, as platforms to publish articles that criticized lower-level government officials or discredited "Western" ideas, such as pop culture and globalization.

A few purportedly independent websites consistently reported the government's viewpoint. Government-owned media, such as the UzA and Jahon Information Agencies, frequently carried reports about reforms or visits to the country in which foreign experts' comments were misquoted or embellished.

<u>Violence and Harassment</u>: Police and security services subjected print and broadcast journalists to arrest, harassment, intimidation, and violence, as well as to bureaucratic restrictions on their activity.

As in past years, the government harassed journalists from state-run and independent media outlets in retaliation for unauthorized contact with foreign diplomats, specifically questioning journalists about such contact. Some journalists refused to meet with foreign diplomats face-to-face because doing so in the past resulted in harassment and questioning by the NSS.

In June 2015 authorities detained Barnokhon Khudoyarova, editor in chief of the *Huquq Dunyosi* (*World of Law*) newspaper, shortly after he wrote a critical article on the Narin District Prosecutor's Office and State Tax Committee. In October 2015 the Narin District Criminal Court found her guilty of extortion and sentenced her to five years four months in prison. In December 2015 the Namangan Regional Criminal Court declined an appeal and kept the sentence without changes.

<u>Censorship or Content Restrictions</u>: Journalists and senior editorial staff in state media organizations reported that some officials' responsibilities included censorship. In many cases, the government placed individuals as editors in chief with the expressed intent that they serve as the main censor for a particular media outlet. There continued to be reports that government officials and employers provided verbal directives to journalists to refrain from covering certain events sponsored by foreign embassies, and, in some cases, threatened termination for noncompliance. As in past years, regional television outlets broadcast some moderately critical stories on local issues, such as water, electricity, and gas shortages, as well as corruption and pollution.

The government continued to refuse Radio Free Europe/Radio Liberty, Voice of America, and the BBC World Service permission to broadcast from within the country, although the websites of Voice of America and the BBC were periodically accessible.

Government security services and other offices regularly directed publishers to print articles and letters under fictitious bylines and gave explicit instructions about the types of stories permitted for publication. There was often little distinction between the editorial content of a government and a privately owned newspaper. Journalists engaged in little investigative reporting. Widely read tabloids occasionally published articles that presented mild criticism of government policies or discussed some problems that the government considered sensitive, such as trafficking in persons.

Journalists working for state media outlets were discouraged from attending events held at foreign embassies.

<u>Libel/Slander Laws</u>: The criminal and administrative codes impose significant fines for libel and defamation. The government used charges of libel, slander, and defamation to punish journalists, human rights activists, and others who criticized the president or the government.

Internet Freedom

The government generally allowed access to the internet, including social media sites. Internet service providers, allegedly at the government's request, routinely blocked access to websites or certain pages of websites that the government considered objectionable, such as Fergananews.com, Ozodlik.org, and Asiaterra.info. The government blocked several domestic and international news websites and those operated by opposition political parties.

The media law defines websites as media outlets, requiring them to register with authorities and provide the names of their founder, chief editor, and staff members. Websites were not required to submit hard copies of publications to the government.

According to government statistics, approximately 39 percent of individuals in the country used the internet. Unofficial estimates, especially of internet access through mobile communications devices, were higher. Several active online forums allowed registered users to post comments and read discussions on a range of social problems. To become a registered user in these forums, individuals must provide personally identifiable information. It was not clear whether the government attempted to collect this information, although new provisions of the Law on Information Technologies require internet cafe proprietors to log customers' browser history.

A decree requires all websites seeking the ".uz" domain to register with the government's Agency for Press and Information. The decree generally affected only government-owned or government-controlled websites. Opposition websites and those operated by international NGOs or media outlets tended to have domain names registered outside the country.

The government intermittently restricted access to several internet messenger services, sometimes for several months, requiring a proxy server to access services such as Skype, Viber, and Telegram.

Academic Freedom and Cultural Events

The government continued to limit academic freedom and cultural events. Authorities occasionally required department head approval for university lectures, and university professors generally practiced self-censorship.

Although a decree prohibits cooperation between higher educational institutions and foreign entities without the explicit approval of the government, foreign institutions often were able to obtain such approval through the Ministry for Foreign Affairs, especially for foreign-language projects. Some school and university administrations, however, continued to pressure teachers and students to refrain from participating in conferences sponsored by diplomatic missions.

b. Freedom of Peaceful Assembly and Association

Freedom of Assembly

The constitution and law provide for freedom of assembly, but the government often restricted this right. Authorities have the right to suspend or prohibit rallies, meetings, and demonstrations for security reasons. The government often did not grant the permits required for demonstrations. Authorities subjected citizens to large fines, threats, arbitrary detention, and abuse for violating procedures for organizing meetings, rallies, and demonstrations or for facilitating unsanctioned events by providing space, other facilities, or materials. Organizers of "mass events" with the potential for more than 100 participants must sign agreements with the Ministry of Interior for the provision of security prior to advertising or holding such an event. This regulation was broadly applied, even to private corporate functions.

Authorities dispersed and occasionally detained persons involved in peaceful protests and sometimes pressed administrative charges following protest actions. Authorities repeatedly detained such activists as Elena Urlaeva, Malokhat Eshonkulova, and Chamangul Negmanova for attempting to protest outside government buildings for fair elections and government action to redress citizen grievances. In December, the government did permit Urlaeva to protest outside of government buildings on two occasions without incident.

Freedom of Association

While the law provides for freedom of association, the government continued to restrict this right. The government sought to control NGO activity and expressed concerns about internationally funded NGOs and unregulated Islamic and minority religious groups. The operating environment for independent civil society, in particular human right defenders, remained restrictive. Activists reported ongoing government control and harassment.

The Ministry of Justice, which oversees the registration of NGOs, requires NGOs to obtain the ministry's approval to hold meetings with nonmembers, including foreigners; to seek the ministry's clearance on any event materials to be distributed; and to notify the ministry in writing of the content and scope of the events in question.

There are legal restrictions on the types of groups that may be formed, and the law requires that all organizations be registered formally with the government. Authorities used registration requirements to bar foreign NGOs from the country. The law allows for a six-month grace period for new organizations to operate while awaiting registration from the Ministry of Justice, during which time the government officially classifies them as "initiative groups." Several NGOs continued to function as initiative groups for periods longer than six months.

NGOs intending to address sensitive issues, such as HIV/AIDS or refugee problems, often faced increased difficulties in obtaining registration. The government allowed nonpolitical associations and social organizations to register, but complex rules and a cumbersome bureaucracy further complicated the process and created opportunities for government obstruction. The government compelled most local NGOs to join a government-controlled NGO association that allowed the government considerable oversight over their funding and activities. The government required NGOs to coordinate their training sessions or seminars with government authorities. NGO managers believed this stipulation created a way for the government to require prior official permission for all NGO program activities. The government claimed these regulations were intended to simplify registration requirements and lower registration fees, but independent civil society groups reported these requirements had not simplified registration procedures.

The degree to which NGOs were able to operate varied by region because some local officials were more tolerant of NGO activities, particularly when coordinated with government agencies. Civil society groups reported that authorities imposed restrictions after groups had registered, such as requiring advance permission from the Justice Ministry for many public activities.

The administrative liability code imposes large fines for violations of procedures governing NGO activity as well as for "involving others" in "illegal NGOs"; the law does not specify whether the term refers to NGOs suspended or closed by the government or merely NGOs not officially registered. The administrative code also imposes penalties against international NGOs for engaging in political activities, activities inconsistent with their charters, or activities the government did not approve in advance.

The government continued to enforce the 2004 banking decree, ostensibly designed to combat money laundering, which complicated efforts by registered and unregistered NGOs to receive outside funding. The Finance Ministry required humanitarian aid and technical assistance recipients to submit information about their bank transactions. The Ministry of Justice required NGOs to submit detailed reports every six months on any grant funding received, events conducted, and events planned for the next six months. NGO leaders may be fined for conducting events without explicit permission from the ministry, and the fine was several times higher than for some criminal offenses.

Parliament's Public Fund for the Support of Nongovernmental, Noncommercial Organizations, and Other Civil Society Institutions continued to conduct grant competitions to implement primarily socioeconomic projects. Some civil society organizations criticized the fund for primarily supporting government-organized NGOs. The law criminalizes membership in organizations the government broadly deemed "extremist."

c. Freedom of Religion

See the Department of State's *International Religious Freedom Report* at www.state.gov/religiousfreedomreport/.

d. Freedom of Movement, Internally Displaced Persons, Protection of Refugees, and Stateless Persons

The constitution and laws provide for freedom of internal movement, foreign travel, emigration, and repatriation, but the government limited these rights, in particular through the continued requirement for citizens to receive an exit visa for travel outside the Commonwealth of Independent States (CIS).

In-country Movement: Citizens were required to have a domicile registration stamp in their passport before traveling domestically or leaving the country, and the government at times delayed domestic and foreign travel and emigration during the visa application process. Permission from local authorities was required to move to Tashkent City or the Tashkent Region; given the narrow scope of the ground for Tashkent registration, authorities rarely granted such permission without the payment of bribes. Those living and working without Tashkent City or

Tashkent Region registration were unable to receive city services and could not legally work, send their children to school, or receive routine medical care.

The government required hotels to register foreign visitors with the government on a daily basis. Foreigners staying in private homes were required to register their location within three days of arrival. Government officials closely monitored foreigners in border areas, but foreigners generally could move within the country without restriction.

Foreign Travel: The government occasionally closed borders around national holidays due to security concerns. The government generally granted the requisite exit visas for citizens and foreign permanent residents to travel or emigrate outside the CIS. Exit visa procedures, however, allow authorities to deny travel based on "information demonstrating the inexpedience of the travel." According to civil society activists, these provisions were poorly defined and denials could not be appealed. Authorities sometimes interfered in foreign travel if the purpose of the trip was expressly religious in nature. There were reports of significant delays in the issuance of new passports, which reportedly could be reduced with bribes.

The government requires male relatives of women between the ages of 18 and 35 to submit a statement pledging that the women would not engage in illegal behavior, including prostitution while abroad, a regulation the government says is aimed at combating trafficking in persons. Observers noted, however, that the majority of Uzbek trafficking victims abroad were male victims of labor trafficking.

Although the law requires authorities to reach a decision on issuing exit visas within 15 days, the government reportedly delayed exit visas for human rights activists and independent journalists to prevent their travel. Authorities continued to deny exit visas to human rights activists Shukhrat Rustamov, Uktam Pardaev, Elena Urlaeva, Adelaida Kim, Khaitboy Yakubov, and others. Violating rules for exiting or entering the country is punishable by imprisonment of five to 10 years.

While citizens generally could travel to neighboring states, land travel to Afghanistan remained difficult because citizens needed permission from the NSS.

Emigration and Repatriation: The law does not provide for dual citizenship and requires returning citizens to be able to prove they did not acquire foreign citizenship while abroad or face loss of citizenship. Citizens possessing dual citizenship did not have recourse to benefits granted by foreign citizenship while in Uzbekistan but generally traveled without impediment if they followed Uzbek law.

The government noted that citizens residing outside the country for more than six months could voluntarily register with Uzbekistan's consulates.

According to the 2015 amendments to the Law on Citizenship, the state can revoke citizenship of those citizens who cause harm to the interests of the society and state; engage in activities in favor of a foreign state; or commit crimes against peace and security. Information regarding the implementation and impact of these amendments, including the number of those whose citizenship was revoked was not provided by the government.

Protection of Refugees

Access to Asylum: The laws do not provide for the granting of asylum or refugee status, and the government has not established a system for providing protection to refugees.

Refoulement: The government provided some protection against the expulsion or return of refugees to countries where their lives or freedom would be threatened due to their race, religion, nationality, membership in a particular social group, or political opinion.

In the absence of a resident Office of the UN High Commissioner for Refugees (UNHCR), the UN Development Program (UNDP) continued to assist with monitoring and resettlement processing of 18 pending (predominantly Afghan) refugee cases involving 27 individuals; such cases predated the closure of the local UNHCR office in 2006. During the year UNDP and temporary duty UNHCR staff processed five cases involving seven persons. Because the UNDP does not process new claims or make refugee status determinations, it referred potential applicants to UNHCR offices in neighboring countries.

The government did not accept UNHCR mandate certificates as a basis for extended legal residence; persons carrying such certificates must apply for either tourist visas or residence permits or face possible deportation. Residence permits were difficult to obtain. The government considered UNHCR mandate refugees from Afghanistan and Tajikistan to be economic migrants, and officials occasionally subjected them to harassment and demands for bribes. Most refugees from Tajikistan were ethnic Uzbeks. Unlike refugees from Afghanistan, those from Tajikistan were able to integrate into the local communities, and the local population supported them.

Stateless Persons

Some refugees from Tajikistan were officially stateless or faced the possibility of becoming officially stateless, as many carried only old Soviet passports rather than Tajik or Uzbek passports. Children born to two stateless parents could receive Uzbek citizenship only if both parents had a residence permit.

Although official data on the number of stateless persons was not available, authoritative human rights activists estimated there were 3,000 stateless persons in Khorezm Province and the autonomous Republic of Karakalpakstan. Most of these individuals reportedly were women who had married and lived in neighboring Turkmenistan prior to the country's independence in 1991. There also were reports of stateless populations in Sirdaryo and Qashkadaryo Provinces. There were reports of authorities revoking citizenship for ethnic Tajiks on allegations of fraud, even in cases where Uzbek passports had been issued more than a decade ago, rendering such citizens stateless.

Section 3. Freedom to Participate in the Political Process

While the constitution and law provide citizens the ability to choose their government in free and fair periodic elections held by secret ballot and based on universal and equal suffrage, the government in practice did not conduct free and fair elections, severely restricted freedom of expression, and suppressed political opposition. The former president oversaw a highly centralized government through sweeping decree powers, primary authority for drafting legislation, and control over government appointments, most of the economy, and the security forces.

Elections and Political Participation

Recent Elections: Following elections in March 2015, President Karimov began a fourth consecutive term, despite Article 90 of the constitution that prohibits more than two consecutive terms in office. Karimov passed away on September 2 and a special presidential election took place on December 4. Acting Interim President and Prime Minister Shavkat Mirziyoyev won the election with 88 percent of the vote. Mirziyoyev was one of four candidates that ran for election. OSCE/ODHIR has observed six elections in Uzbekistan, however 2016 was the first time the

Uzbek government invited OSCE/ODHIR to conduct a full-scope observation mission. According to OSCE/ODHIR, the 2016 presidential election demonstrated that systemic shortcomings in the election system persist and the dominant position of state actors and limits on fundamental freedoms continue to undermine political pluralism. These conditions resulted in a campaign that lacked genuine competition. Furthermore, due to a highly restrictive and controlled media environment, voters did not have access to alternate viewpoints beyond a state-defined narrative. The OSCE/ODHIR report indicated that significant irregularities were noted on election day, including indications of ballot box stuffing and widespread proxy voting. The report also identified an increased transparency in the election, service to disabled voters, and unfettered access for 600 international observers.

Political Parties and Political Participation: The law allows independent political parties, but the Ministry of Justice has broad powers to oversee parties and to withhold financial and legal support to those they judge to be opposed to the government. There are four registered political parties and four candidates representing each party ran in the December 4 special presidential election. The law makes it difficult for genuinely independent political parties to organize, nominate candidates, and campaign. The law allows the Ministry of Justice to suspend parties for as long as six months without a court order. The government also exercised control over established parties by controlling their financing and media exposure.

The OSCE/ODHIR observation mission found that the campaign lacked competitiveness and voters lacked a genuine choice of political alternatives. Candidates can only be nominated by a registered political party and must meet certain eligibility criteria. Candidate cannot self-nominate. The government lowered the number of supporting signatures needed for candidate registration this year from five percent to one percent of voters nationwide. The OSCE/ODHIR also noted that the campaign was moderately visible, but campaign materials were largely homogenous. There were no debates among the candidates themselves.

The law prohibits judges, public prosecutors, NSS officials, members of the armed forces, foreign citizens, and stateless persons from joining political parties. The law prohibits parties that are based on religion or ethnicity; oppose the sovereignty, integrity, or security of the country, or the constitutional rights and freedoms of citizens; promote war or social, national, or religious hostility; or seek to overthrow the government. The law also prohibits the Islamist political organization Hizb-ut-Tahrir, stating it promotes hate and condones acts of terrorism.

The government banned or denied registration to several political parties following the 2005 violence in Andijon. Former party leaders remained in exile, and their parties struggled to remain relevant without a strong domestic base.

<u>Participation of Women and Minorities</u>: No laws limit the participation of women and members of minorities in the political process, and they did participate. National minorities have full political rights under the Constitution and campaign materials were available in minority languages. The Central Election Commission passed a regulation in 2016, ensuring persons with disabilities could access polling stations and vote.

Section 4. Corruption and Lack of Transparency in Government

In December 2016, the Uzbek parliament approved a new law to fight corruption. The law strengthens criminal penalties for official corruption. Despite some high-level corruption-related arrests, corruption remained endemic, and officials frequently engaged in corrupt practices with impunity. According to local observers, prosecutions often targeted potential competitors for economic resources who had lost support among local and national elites, and such prosecutions were not the result of a concerted effort to stamp out corruption.

<u>Corruption</u>: In February Radio Ozodlik, RFE/RL's Uzbek Service, reported that the head of the Ministry of Defense department in Pskent District, Major Sodik Nishanov, was sentenced to four and one-half years in prison. His subordinates, Ibrakhim Kirgizbaev, Jasur Atamuradov, and Ilkhom Amanov, received five and one-half, three, and two years, respectively. According to the radio's sources, the officers were found guilty of engaging in fraud and taking and receiving bribes.

In May, Ozodlik reported that former Hokim (mayor) of Andijon Nurillo Alimov was sentenced to 18 years in prison for a number of offenses, including abuse of power and bribery.

Interim President Shavkat Mirziyoyev appointed Abdulla Aripov in September as Deputy Prime Minister and in December promoted him to Prime Minister. Aripov had been the subject of criminal charges for corruption in 2012 reportedly for granting a foreign cellular company permits to install antennas and had been dismissed from office by late president Karimov, though some speculate that the charges reflected internal political considerations rather than his complicity or culpability.

Financial Disclosure: Government officials are required to disclose only income from outside employment, and such disclosures were not publicly available.

Public Access to Information: The public did not generally have access to government information, although the government launched an interactive website enabling citizens to file complaints and seek redress for grievances. The government seldom reported information normally considered in the public domain. Many government ministries and bodies had an internet presence that offered some information. In accordance with the law on Openness and Transparency of State Bodies, citizens may attend nonsensitive government meetings. State bodies should make public announcements on their meetings no later than three days prior to the date of the event. Any person then can file a registration request (indicating his full name and address) and attend the meeting if the request is approved. Attending citizens can ask questions related to the topic of the meeting, but there is a ban on video and audio recording.

Section 5. Governmental Attitude Regarding International and Nongovernmental Investigation of Alleged Violations of Human Rights

A number of domestic human rights groups operated in the country, although the government often hampered their activities in a variety of ways. The government frequently harassed, arrested, abused, and prosecuted human rights activists. There were continued reports that law enforcement officers strictly controlled activists around the September 1 Independence Day holiday, the December 8 Constitution Day holiday, and the May 13 anniversary of the Andijon events.

The government officially acknowledged two domestic human rights NGOs: Ezgulik and the Independent Human Rights Organization of Uzbekistan. Ezgulik representatives reported that the authorities' harassment, intimidation, and threats of judicial proceedings against members continued to hamper their activities throughout the country. Others were unable to register but continued to function at both the national and local levels.

Organizations that attempted to register in previous years and remained unregistered included the Human Rights Alliance, Najot, Humanitarian Legal Center, Human Rights Society of Uzbekistan, the Expert Working Group, and Mazlum (Oppressed). These organizations did not exist as legal entities but continued to function, despite difficulty renting offices and conducting financial transactions. They could not open bank accounts, making it virtually impossible for them to receive funds. Unregistered groups were vulnerable to government prosecution. In certain cases, however, government representatives participated with unregistered groups in events.

Government officials spoke informally with domestic human rights defenders, some of whom were able to resolve cases of human rights abuses through direct engagement with authorities if they did not publicize these cases.

Occasional attacks against human rights activists continued. Human rights defenders repeatedly alleged they were subject to spurious criminal and administrative charges and other retribution in response to their activism.

The United Nations or Other International Bodies: With the exception of the International Labor Organization (ILO), the government continued to restrict the work of international bodies and severely criticized their human rights monitoring activities and policies.

The OSCE has been able to do limited work on human rights problems since 2006, and the government approved several proposed OSCE projects during the year, including in the "human dimension," the human rights component of the OSCE's work.

The government has not permitted UN representatives to monitor human rights problems in the country for more than 10 years, despite numerous requests. The government never responded to a 2006 request by the UN Office of the High Commissioner for Human Rights, and 11 other human rights-related UN special mandate holders and working groups still had unanswered applications for entry at year's end.

Government Human Rights Bodies: The goals of the Human Rights Ombudsman's Office included promoting observance and public awareness of fundamental human rights, assisting in shaping legislation to bring it into accordance with international human rights norms, and resolving cases of alleged abuse. The Ombudsman's Office mediated disputes between citizens who contacted it and made recommendations to modify or uphold decisions of government agencies, but its recommendations were not binding. Families of prisoners of concern reported that the Ombudsman's Office declined to engage on politically sensitive cases.

The National Human Rights Center (NHRC) is a government agency responsible for educating the public and officials on the principles of human rights and democracy and for ensuring that the government complied with its international obligations to provide human rights information. Observers noted, however, that the NHRC was largely ineffective in this role and that it focused more on defending the government's record on human rights than on addressing human rights problems.

Section 6. Discrimination, Societal Abuses, and Trafficking in Persons

Women

Rape and Domestic Violence: The law prohibits rape, including rape of a "close relative," but the criminal code does not specifically prohibit spousal rape, and the courts did not try any cases. Cultural norms discouraged women and their families from speaking openly about rape, and the press rarely reported it.

The law does not specifically prohibit domestic violence, which remained common. While the law punishes physical assault, police often discouraged women in particular from making complaints against abusive partners, and officials rarely removed abusers from their homes or took them into custody. Society considered the physical abuse of women to be a personal rather than criminal matter. Human rights contacts, however, reported greater willingness by local police and officials to address reports of domestic violence, including in Jizzakh Province and in the traditionally conservative Fergana Valley. Family members or elders usually handled such cases, and they rarely came to court. Local authorities emphasized reconciling husband and wife, rather than addressing the abuse.

There were no government-run shelters or hotlines for victims of domestic abuse, and few NGOs focused on domestic violence.

Sexual Harassment: The law does not explicitly prohibit sexual harassment, but it is illegal for a male supervisor to coerce a woman who has a business or financial dependency into a sexual relationship. Social norms, lack of reporting, and lack of legal recourse made it difficult to assess the scope of the problem.

Reproductive Rights: Couples and individuals generally have the right to decide freely and responsibly the number, spacing, and timing of their children; to manage their reproductive health; and to have the information and means to do so, free from discrimination, coercion, and violence. There were reports that government doctors pressured women to accept birth control or employ medical measures, such as sterilization, to end the possibility of pregnancy, purportedly to control the birth rate and reduce infant and maternal mortality. Contacts in the human rights and health-care communities confirmed there was anecdotal evidence suggesting that sterilizations without informed consent occurred, although it was unclear whether the practice was widespread and whether senior government officials directed it.

Contraception generally was available to men and women. In most districts, maternity clinics were available and staffed by fully trained doctors, who gave a wide range of prenatal and postpartum care. There were reports that more women in rural areas than in urban areas gave birth at home without the presence of skilled medical attendants.

Discrimination: Legal status and rights are the same for men and women. The National Women's Committee is tasked with promoting the legal rights of women. Women historically held leadership positions across many sectors of society, although they were not as prevalent as men, and cultural and religious practices limited their effectiveness. The government provided little data that could be used to determine whether women experienced discrimination in access to employment or credit or were paid less for substantially similar work. The labor code prohibits women from working in many industries open to men.

Children

Birth Registration: Citizenship is derived by birth within the country's territory or from one's parents. The government generally registered all births immediately.

Medical Care: While the government provided equal subsidized health care for boys and girls, those without an officially registered address, such as street children and children of migrant workers, did not have access to government health facilities.

Child Abuse: Society generally considered child abuse to be an internal family matter; little official information was available on the subject.

Early and Forced Marriage: The minimum legal age for marriage is 17 for women and 18 for men, although a district may lower the age by one year in exceptional cases. The government-run Women's Committee and neighborhood (mahalla) representatives conducted systematic campaigns to raise awareness of the dangers of child marriage and early births. The committee also held regular public meetings with community representatives and girls in schools to emphasize the importance of education, self-reliance, financial independence, and the right to free choice. In some rural areas, girls as young as 15 were married in religious ceremonies not officially recognized by the state.

Sexual Exploitation of Children: The law seeks to protect children from "all forms of exploitation." Involving a child in prostitution is punishable by a fine of 25 to 50 times the minimum monthly salary and imprisonment for up to five years.

The minimum age for consensual sex is 16. The punishment for statutory rape is 15 to 20 years' imprisonment. The production, exhibition, and/or distribution of child pornography (involving persons younger than age 21) is punishable by fine or by imprisonment for up to three years.

International Child Abductions: The country is a party to the 1980 Hague Convention on the Civil Aspects of International Child Abduction. See the Department of State's *Annual Report on International Parental Child Abduction* at travel.state.gov/content/childabduction/en/legal/compliance.html.

Anti-Semitism

There were no reports of anti-Semitic acts or patterns of discrimination against Jews. The Jewish community was unable to meet the registration requirements necessary to have a centrally registered organization, but there were eight registered Jewish congregations. Observers estimated the Jewish population at 10,000, concentrated mostly in Tashkent, Samarkand, and Bukhara. Their numbers continued to decline due to emigration, largely for economic reasons.

Trafficking in Persons

See the Department of State's *Trafficking in Persons Report* at www.state.gov/j/tip/rls/tiprpt/.

Persons with Disabilities

The law prohibits discrimination against persons with disabilities, but societal discrimination on the basis of disability occurred.

The government continued efforts to confirm the disability levels of citizens who received government disability benefits, claiming it did so to ensure the legitimacy of disability payments. Unconfirmed reports suggested, however, that authorities unfairly reduced benefits to some individuals in the process.

The law allows for fines if buildings, including private shops and restaurants, are not accessible, and activists reported that authorities fined individuals or organizations in approximately 2,500 cases during the year. A 2013 law reduced the fine for failing to create the necessary conditions for persons with disabilities from 6.4 to 9.2 million som ($1,960 to $2,817) to 2.2 million som ($674). Disability activists reported that accessibility remained inadequate, noting, for example, that many of the high schools constructed in recent years had exterior ramps but no interior modifications to facilitate access by wheelchair users.

The Ministry of Health controlled access to health care for persons with disabilities, and the Ministry of Labor facilitated employment of persons with disabilities. No information was available regarding patterns of abuse in educational and mental health facilities.

The labor law states that all citizens enjoy equal employment rights, but disability rights activists reported that discrimination occurred and estimated that 90 percent of persons with disabilities were unemployed. The government indicated 17,000 jobs were set aside for persons with disabilities and during the reporting period, the authorities provided employment for over 4,000 disabled citizens. The government mandates that social infrastructure sites, urban and residential areas, airports, railway stations, and other facilities must allow for disabled access, although there were no specific government programs implemented and activists reported particular difficulties with access. Activists also reported instances in which persons with disabilities were not provided sign language interpreters during police investigations and court hearings, though the government did provide Braille ballots during the December election.

According to the government, of the children under 16 with disabilities in the country, 30,122 attended public schools, 6,225 attended specialized schools, and 9,499 were home schooled. Students studied Braille books published during Soviet times. There were computers adapted for people with vision disabilities.

National/Racial/Ethnic Minorities

The country had significant Tajik (5 percent) and Russian (5.5 percent) minorities, as well as smaller Kazakh, Korean, and Kyrgyz minorities. There was also a small Romani (locally known as Lyuli) population, estimated at fewer than 50,000 individuals. Complaints of societal violence or discrimination against members of these groups were rare.

Ethnic Russians and other minorities occasionally expressed concern about limited job opportunities. Officials reportedly reserved senior positions in the government bureaucracy and business for ethnic Uzbeks, although there were numerous exceptions.

The law does not require Uzbek language ability to obtain citizenship, but language often was a sensitive issue. Uzbek is the state language, and the constitution requires that the president speak it. The law also provides that Russian is "the language of interethnic communication."

Acts of Violence, Discrimination, and Other Abuses Based on Sexual Orientation and Gender Identity

Sexual relations between men are punishable by up to three years' imprisonment. Although there have not been any known arrests or convictions under this provision since 2003, according to members of the lesbian, gay, bisexual, transgender, and intersex (LGBTI) community, police and other law enforcement personnel used the threat of arrest or prosecution to extract heavy bribes from gay men. According to Ozodlik Radio, RFE/RL's Uzbek Service, a video released in January showing police officers beating a transvestite male allegedly involved in prostitution was distributed through social media outlets and messengers. Ozodlik reported that two police officers were dismissed for abuse of power. In response to questions regarding the case, the government confirmed the "dismissal of interior affairs officials responsible for illegal actions against a perpetrator." The law does not criminalize same-sex sexual activity between women.

On February 5, Uzbek state-owned First TV channel O`zbekiston broadcast a February 4 speech by then president Islam Karimov at a special session of Tashkent Regional Council of People's Deputies in which he openly denounced homosexuals and criticized Western culture for "propagating" such lifestyles, claiming "there is something wrong" with them. Ozodlik Radio also reported that Karimov criticized same-sex relationships during the speech.

Same-sex sexual activity was generally a taboo subject in society, and there were no known LGBTI organizations. There were no reports of official or societal discrimination based on sexual orientation or gender identity in employment, housing, statelessness, or access to education or health care, but observers attributed the absence of such reports principally to the social taboo against discussing same-sex relationships.

HIV and AIDS Social Stigma

Persons known to be HIV positive reported social isolation and discrimination by public agency workers, health personnel, law enforcement officers, landlords, and employers after their HIV status became known. The military summarily expelled recruits in the armed services found to be HIV positive. Some LGBTI community activists reported that hospital wards reviewed the personal history of HIV-infected patients and categorized them as being drug addicts, homosexuals, or engaged in prostitution. Those whose files were marked as "homosexual" were referred to the police for investigation, because homosexuality between men is a criminal act. The government's restrictions on local NGOs left only a handful of functioning NGOs to assist and protect the rights of persons with HIV/AIDS. No credible demographic or health survey data dealing with HIV/AIDS was publicly available.

Section 7. Worker Rights

a. Freedom of Association and the Right to Collective Bargaining

The law generally provides the right of workers to form and join independent unions and bargain collectively. The law does not make clear that only in the absence of a trade union can other bodies elected by workers be given the authority to bargain collectively. The law neither provides for nor prohibits the right to strike. The law prohibits anti-union discrimination. The law on trade unions states that workers cannot be fired due to trade union membership, but it does not clearly state whether workers fired for union activity must be reinstated. Volunteers in public works and workers employed by individuals without documented contracts do not have legal protection.

The government did not effectively enforce applicable laws, and there were no independent unions. Article 200 of the Administrative Responsibility Code and article 217 of the Criminal Code provide penalties for violating freedom of association laws equal to five to 10 times the minimum salary. Resources, inspections, and remediation were inadequate, and the law provided for no penalties for violations of the rights to freedom of association and collective bargaining. In October, the country ratified ILO Convention 87 (Freedom of Association and the Right to Organize), and amended the law on "professional unions, rights, and guarantees of their activities," which improved the role of the trade unions in the protection of labor and employees' social rights. Workers generally did not exercise their right to form and join unions due to fear that attempts to create alternative unions would be quickly repressed. Unions remained centralized and wholly dependent on the government.

The state-run Federation of Trade Unions of Uzbekistan incorporated more than 35,800 primary organizations and 14 regional trade unions; according to official reports, 60 percent of employees in the country participated in the federation. Leaders of the federation were appointed by the President's Office rather than elected by the union members or board. All regional and industrial trade unions at the local level were state managed.

Unions and their leaders were not free to conduct activities without interference from their employer or from government-controlled institutions. Unions were government-organized institutions with little bargaining power aside from some influence on health and work safety issues, and workers did not exercise collective bargaining rights. For example, the Ministry of Labor and the Ministry of Finance, in consultation with the Federation of Trade Unions, set wages for government employees. In the emerging private sector, management established wages or negotiated them individually with persons who contracted for employment. There was no state institution responsible for labor arbitration.

b. Prohibition of Forced or Compulsory Labor

The law prohibits all forms of forced or compulsory labor, except as legal punishment for such offenses as robbery, fraud, or tax evasion or as specified by law. Certain sections of the Criminal Code and Code of Administrative Offenses allow for compulsory labor as a punishment for offenses including defamation; incitement of national, racial, ethnic, or religious enmity; creation or participation in the activity of prohibited social associations and religious organizations; and violation of the procedure for the organization and conducting of assemblies, meetings, street processions, or demonstrations. In multiple instances, the government pursued complaints of forced labor, even those from independent observers, which resulted in prosecutions, administrative penalties, and fines of seven local officials accused of forcing people to work. In 2016 the government made efforts to inform the public about the prohibition against forced labor, including the annual cotton harvest. The ILO verified that the government of Uzbekistan achieved some progress towards the eradication of adult forced labor in the cotton harvest as shown by decreasing numbers of people directly coerced to pick cotton, but effective prevention was irregular and risks of forced labor still remain.

Government-compelled forced labor of adults remained endemic during the annual cotton harvest. The central government continued to demand farmers and local officials fulfill state-assigned cotton production quotas and set insufficiently low prices for cotton and labor to attract voluntary workers, which led to the wide-scale mobilizations of adult laborers and a smaller number of child laborers. The government also continued to conceal possible labor violations in cotton fields by aggressively confronting, harassing, and detaining independent monitors attempting to observe and document the harvest. Adults were expected to pick 120 to 154 pounds per day, with the resulting daily wage between 15,400 to 18,200 som ($4.72 to $5.57) per day. While the earnings' dollar equivalents were offered at the official government rate, at the prevailing black market rate used in the country due to the difficulty with obtaining official conversion, dollar equivalent earnings were approximately half of those at the official rate. The government for the first time announced that it did not meet its annual quota. Working conditions varied greatly by region and farm. There continued to be scattered reports of inadequate food and lodging, and some students reportedly worked the harvest without access to clean drinking water. The scope of adult mobilizations differed significantly from region to region.

For the third consecutive year, the government effectively forbade the systemic mobilization of children under age 18, although there were isolated reports of some local officials mobilizing classes of students ages 14 to 16 years in the final weeks of the harvest.

Despite official statements that the government would prohibit the mobilization of teachers and doctors in the 2016 harvest, such mobilizations continued. Independent reports suggested that the forced mobilization of adult state workers during the cotton harvest increased during the year to compensate for the loss of underage workers. Authorities continued to expect many teachers and school administrators to participate in the harvest, as either supervisors or cotton pickers. The majority of schools, colleges, and lyceums remained open with a reduced faculty, but there were reports of colleges closing or cancelling classes in certain regions due to staffing shortages. Similar conditions prevailed in the medical sector, as hospitals and clinics were understaffed for much of the cotton season.

The loss of public-sector workers during the cotton harvest adversely affected communities, as medical procedures often were deferred and essential public services delayed.

There were isolated reports stating that local officials forced farmers to cultivate silk cocoons and, separately, that local officials forced teachers, students (including children), private businesses employees, and others to work in construction and other forms of non-cotton agriculture and to clean parks, streets, and buildings.

Also see the Department of State's *Trafficking in Persons Report* at www.state.gov/j/tip/rls/tiprpt/.

c. Prohibition of Child Labor and Minimum Age for Employment

The law sets the minimum working age at 16 and provides that work must not interfere with the studies of those younger than 18. The law establishes a right to part-time light work beginning at age 15, and children with permission from their parents may work a maximum of 24 hours per week when school is not in session and 12 hours per week when school is in session. The law does not allow children under age 15 to be involved with "light work," even if it does not interfere with education or hinder the health or development of the child, but this provision was not always observed. Children between ages 16 and 18 may work 36 hours per week while school is out of session and 18 hours per week while school is in session. Decrees stipulate a list of hazardous activities forbidden for children younger than age 18 and prohibit employers from using children to work under specified hazardous conditions, including underground, underwater, at dangerous heights, and in the manual harvesting of cotton, including cotton harvesting with dangerous equipment. Children were employed in agriculture, in family businesses such as bakeries and convenience stores, and as street vendors.

The law does not explicitly provide authority for inspectors from the Ministry of Labor to enforce the child labor laws, which is a shared responsibility of the Ministry of Labor, the prosecutor general, the Ministry of Interior, and the Ministry of Interior's general criminal investigators. The Office of the Prime Minister took the lead role in coordinating enforcement of labor decrees to keep children out of cotton fields and in mobilizing health and education workers. Local officials often reportedly participated by forming monitoring groups to ensure that parents and schools did not allow their children to pick cotton. It was unclear whether the Ministry of Interior conducted inspections in the agricultural sector. The law allows for a fine in the amount of one to three minimal monthly salaries for those using child labor that could "harm the child's health, safety or morals." There were no known prosecutions for child labor during the year.

During the year the government conducted its own monitoring for child labor in the cotton sector using ILO methodology in Navoi, Surkhandaryo, and Khorezm regions, and an ILO-led mission monitored the harvest in the remaining regions and the autonomous Republic of Karakalpakstan. The ILO mission concluded that there was no systemic use of child labor in the harvest, but certain risks of forced labor remain, although a significant number (up to two/thirds) of the cotton pickers work voluntarily and only a minority is recruited involuntarily.

Some students as young as age 10 still worked in the cultivation and picking of cotton; however, unlike in previous years, their presence was the result of localized or individual occurrences rather than nationwide mobilization. The government continued to mobilize third-course college and lyceum students, sometimes for weeks at a time, resulting in the disruption of classes. Most third-course students were generally age 18 or older. There were reports, however, that this practice resulted in the incidental mobilization of 17-year-old students in the same class. Officials at some universities sent students to pick cotton for as long as eight weeks, during which time they stayed in tented work camps or schools near the fields a long distance away from the university. Some activists attempting to monitor living conditions for student workers in these areas reported interference by law enforcement officials, including through physical abuse. As in past years, there were individual reports that educational institutions threatened to expel students who did not participate in the harvest or required students to sign statements indicating their "voluntary" participation in the harvest. During the fall harvest, three professional colleges, two schools, and one clinic were closed to the public to provide accommodation for cotton pickers. Upon receiving complaints, the authorities took corrective measures and open the closed clinic and education facilities.

Also see the Department of Labor's *Findings on the Worst Forms of Child Labor* at www.dol.gov/ilab/reports/child-labor/findings/.

d. Discrimination with Respect to Employment and Occupation

Laws and regulations prohibit discrimination with respect to employment and occupation based on race, gender, religion, and language. The labor code states that differences in the treatment of individuals deserving of the state's protection or requiring special accommodation, including women, children, and persons with disabilities, are not to be considered discriminatory. Laws do not prohibit discrimination on the basis of sexual orientation or gender identity, age, political opinion, national origin or citizenship, or social origin. HIV-positive individuals are legally prohibited from being employed in certain occupations, including those in the medical field that require direct contact with patients or with blood or blood products, as well as in cosmetology or haircutting. The government generally did not effectively enforce these laws and regulations. Information on penalties was not readily available. There were no recent reliable data on employment discrimination.

Foreign migrant workers enjoy the same legal protections as Uzbek workers as long as their employers follow all legal procedures for their employment. The law provides for a number of punishments or Uzbek employers who do not follow all legal procedures. Enforcement of employment law was lax, primarily due to insufficient staffing of relevant entities and endemic corruption.

e. Acceptable Conditions of Work

The national minimum monthly wage, used primarily to calculate salaries in the public sector as well as various taxes and duties, was 130,240 som ($40) per month between September 2015 and September 2016. On October 1, it increased 15 percent to 149,775 som ($46). (Due to the difficulty in obtaining official conversion, the real earning power of the minimum monthly wage approximately half of that calculated at the official rate.)

According to official sources, approximately 360,000 full-time employees (out of 12 million) received the minimum salary. In 2013 the president signed an amendment to the labor code that raised the minimum monthly salary for full-time employees in the public sector to 230,000 som ($70). There were no official statistics concerning the average monthly wage, but most experts estimated a figure of 780,000 som ($239) before taxes. This level did not include wages in the agricultural sector. Reliable data or estimates on actual average household income were not available.

Officials defined the poverty level as consumption of fewer than 2,100 calories per day, but the government did not publish any income indicators of poverty. According to the government, 17 percent of the population lived below the poverty level, but some unofficial estimates using different indicators put the figure as high as 77 percent.

The law establishes a standard workweek of 40 hours and requires a 24-hour rest period. The law provides for paid annual holidays. The law provides overtime compensation as specified in employment contracts or as agreed with an employee's trade union. Such compensation can be provided in the form of additional pay or leave. The law states that overtime compensation should not be less than 200 percent of the employee's average monthly salary rate. Additional leave time should not be less than the length of actual overtime work. An employee may not work more than 120 hours of overtime per year, but this limitation was not generally observed, particularly in the public sector. The law prohibits compulsory overtime.

The Ministry of Labor establishes and enforces occupational health and safety standards in consultation with unions. Employers are responsible for ensuring compliance of standards, rules, and regulations on labor protection, as well as obligations under collective agreements. Reports suggested that enforcement was not effective. Although regulations provide for safeguards, workers in hazardous jobs often lacked protective clothing and equipment. Labor inspectors conducted routine inspections of small and medium-sized businesses once every four years and inspected larger enterprises once every three years. Additionally, the ministry or a local governor's office could initiate a selective inspection of a business, and special inspections were conducted in response to accidents or complaints.

Approximately five to eight labor inspectors staffed offices in each of the country's 14 administrative units, and there were specialized offices for major industries, such as construction, mining, and manufacturing. Labor inspectors usually focused on the private sector, while inspections of state-owned enterprises were considered pro forma. Penalties reportedly were often selective, and in many cases employers reportedly were able to mitigate penalties through informal agreements with inspectors. According to the law, health and safety standards should be applied in all sectors. The law remained unenforced in the informal economy, where employment was usually undocumented. During the year the Ministry of Labor, in cooperation with the tax authorities, inspected all private clinics to target the widespread practice of employing specialists without employment contracts.

The government agreed on an extension of the International Labor Organization's (ILO) Decent Work Country Program until 2020, which would lead to further efforts towards improving working conditions. The most common labor violations were working without contracts (1.9 percent), receiving lower than publicly announced payments (.08 percent), delayed payments (1.3 percent), substandard sanitary or hygienic working conditions (14.5 percent). In 2016, acting on citizen complaints, the authorities took corrective action by mandating that 74 farms must improve the working conditions by providing proper contracts, transportation, better sanitary facilities, meals and drinking water, and timely salary payments.

The law provides that workers may legally remove themselves from hazardous work if an employer fails to provide adequate safety measures for the job, and the employer must pay the employee during the time of the work stoppage or provide severance pay if the employee choses to terminate employment. Workers generally did not exercise this right because it was not effectively enforced and employees feared retribution by employers. The law requires employers to insure against civil liability for damage caused to the life or health of an employee in connection with a work injury, occupational disease, or other injury to health caused by the employee's performance on the job. In addition the company's employees have the right to demand and the administration is obliged to provide them with information on the state of working conditions and safety at work, available personal protection means, benefits and compensations. No occupational health and safety violations were reported under the law.

The government and official media did not publish data on the number of employees in the informal economy. Many such employees had official part-time or low-income jobs. There were no effective government programs to provide social protections to workers in the informal economy. Violations of wage, overtime, and occupational health and safety standards were most common in the public sector. More specific information on sectors in which violations were common and specific groups of workers who faced hazardous or exploitative working conditions was not available.